T0352016

THE BRAZILLER SERIES OF AUSTRALIAN POETS

1959   *The Music of Division*, Sydney: Angus & Robertson

1962   *Eight Metropolitan Poems*, Adelaide: Australian Letters;
        with John Brack

1963   *In Light and Darkness*, Sydney: Angus & Robertson

1967   *The Rebel General*, Sydney: Angus & Robertson

1971   *Where the Wind Came*, Sydney: Angus & Robertson

1973   *Selected Poems*, Sydney: Angus & Robertson

1976   *The Foundations of Joy*, (Poets of the Month Series), Sy adney:
        Angus & Robertson

1979   *The Emotions Are Not Skilled Workers*, Sydney: Angus & Robertson

1985   *The Amorous Cannibal*, Oxford: Oxford University Press

1988   *I'm Deadly Serious*, Oxford: Oxford University Press

1989   *Sangue e l'acqua*, translated and edited by Giovann Distefano,
        Abano Terme: Piovan Editore

1990   *For Crying Out Loud*, Oxford: Oxford University Press

1993   *Rungs of Time*, Oxford: Oxford University Press

1995   *Selected Poems 1956–1994*, Oxford: Oxford University Press

1998   *Whirling*, Oxford: Oxford University Press

2001   *By and Large*, Manchester: Carcanet; and Sydney; Brandl
        and Schlesinger

2003   *A Representative Human*, Brunswick: Gungurru Press

2004   *Next*, Brunswick: Gungurru Press

2005   *The Universe Looks Down*, Brandl & Schlesinger

2006   *Then*, Brunswick: Gungurru Press

2008   *Telling a Hawk from a Handsaw*, Manchester Carcanet
        Oxford Poets

2010   *Puck*, Brunswick: Gungurru Press

2012   *New and Selected Poems*, Manchester: Carcanet Oxford Poets

2014   *My Feet Are Hungry*, Sydney: Pitt Street Poets

Afternoon in the Central Nervous System

a selection of poems by

CHRIS WALLACE-CRABBE

WITH A NOTE BY PAUL KANE

GEORGE BRAZILLER / NEW YORK

This Project has been assisted by the Australian Government through the Australia Council for the Arts, its arts funding and advisory body.

George Braziller, Inc.
277 Broadway, Suite 708
New York, NY 10007

Library of Congress Cataloging-in-Publication Dataa
Wallace-Crabbe, Chris.
[Poems. Selections]
Afternoon in the central nervous system a selection of poems / by Chris Wallace-Crabbe ; with a note by Paul Kane.—First edition.
        pages ; cm
ISBN 978-0-8076-0010-8
I. Title.
PR9619.3.W28A6 2015
821.914—dc23
2015014252
ISBN 9780807600108
I. Title.

First edition
Designed by Rita Lascaro
Printed in the United States of America

TABLE OF CONTENTS

In the Introduction to his collection of essays, *Read It Again*, Chris Wallace-Crabbe lets fall the remark that "Poetry has the misfortune to be written in the medium of language." The misfortune, we may say, turns upon the mistaken notion that words are transparent, but the force of his observation lies in the way it calls attention to the fact that poetry, like any other art, is a matter of medium. The poet works with words; their meanings—yes—but also their sound, texture, appearance, their almost tactile effect upon us, the rhythm they make when juxtaposed, even the silence they evoke as an epiphenomenon. In reading Wallace-Crabbe it is useful to bear this in mind because it is at the forefront of his performance even when it appears to take a back seat onstage. When it is front and center, his verse sounds like no one else's:

> Streak, dash, fluff, apricot radiation,
> the whorled blurring of a burned edge:
> solid lavender continents and filiations,
> islands in air, foolishly soft fleeces
> dandled overhead, easterly pinks and peaches
> nervously barred with mauve.
>
> ["Sunset Sky Near Coober Pedy"]

One would not call him Horatian, but Wallace-Crabbe takes to heart Horace's dictum that poetry should delight and instruct, and he is never more delightful than when educative:

> Tears leave no grooves in archaeological sites,
> a broken heart has never been troweled up;
> the lacrimae rerum do not resemble objects
> though misery be as hard as a stone in your hand.
>   ["The Evolution of Tears"]

There are times when one imagines Wallace-Crabbe writing poems in shorts and sandals, so casual is his manner whatever the gravity of his matter. There are few writers as witty or with as coruscating an intellect as he: other more ponderous poets, who seem to grind out their poems, get sparks with flint on steel; Wallace-Crabbe simply strikes a match, then lights a lamp or a fuse. He is a daylight poet, though perfectly at home in the dark. As he says in "Flowing":

> his poems were so full of joy
>   you hardly would dream
>   that the steady encroachment of death
> was his usual theme.

The concern with death gets expressed in tropes of time, including one's own times, where his mordant humor can turn satirical in the service of the long view, as in "A Stone Age Decadent": "Totem and law, laws and unfair totems,/ Banal, sublime, bestial, that's how/ My fellow tribespeople make out the world." When he does address mortality directly, it can be deeply moving. Here is the opening to a poem on the untimely death of his son, where bewilderment over loss is enacted in a momentary perplexity:

> Your girlfriend rang me up today,
> your former girlfriend,
>   no, that isn't right,
> the present friend of all that once was you.
>   ["Erstwhile"]

A genial sophisticate, Wallace-Crabbe is also one of the most insistently *Australian* of Australian poets: his deployment of diction, slang, idiom and local reference constitutes a linguistic and cultural place-making that is deeply local and idiosyncratic. In "Galvo" [galvanized sheet metal] we find "In the backyard/ a creepergrown green dunny" [outhouse], and in "Puck Disembarks" we see how "In his government regulation gear/ And cultural arsy-turvitude/ Puck steps ashore in a grammar of ti-tree" [which requires a separate essay to unpack]. Specifically, Wallace-Crabbe is at home in Melbourne, which, despite the critique of "Melbourne," he manages to domesticate as his *locus amoenus*—where, indeed, the most pleasant place can be the home itself, a domicile for what he terms elsewhere "The Domestic Sublime," where love and truth can be fitted together:

> Someone will push the house over one day,
> Some spacedozer give it a shove,
> But the cobbles we laid down here in the yard,
> These are a labor of love.
> ["Loving in Truth"]

For all the cunning entanglements of his verse, Wallace-Crabbe can be plain-spoken, especially when he wants to speak his mind. This most often occurs when his thinking takes a metaphysical or epistemological turn, as in "We Being Ghosts Cannot Catch Hold of Things," which begins:

> What a piteous quest we have
> to brood upon down here
>
> given that Meaning is a blind god
> who limps through the actual world[.]

In a verse novel of mock-epic dimensions, *The Universe Looks Down*, Wallace-Crabbe explores the whole panoply of his interests, using a series of characters on various quest adventures, both inner and outer. Toward the end of the book he sums up his approach: "My theology's uneven,//Broad-brushy, provisional, post-humanist/ And brightly empirical." Though he is apt to turn theology against itself, that is a quintessential theological move, and there is a sympathetic impulse at work that places him at the threshold that divides and joins the empirical and the religious. This is what enables him to write a wry life of Jesus in "And the Cross," that ends with a humanistic assertion that allows for possibility:

> His legacy? Make your own minds up.
> Did Roman nails deserve his blood?
> Even for someone who venerates money
> Here is a story of absolute good.

In the past, "blood" and "good" once rhymed; we hear it now as an off-rhyme, which itself tropes the liminal space Wallace-Crabbe can occupy, where everything is in motion and nothing finally solidifies. In his poem addressing dust ("which is friend to mankind"), he speaks of the "kindly coverlet of dust" which is:

> like blessing
> or a gray army blanket.
>
> Sweet dust, bless us all in turn.
>   Keep us warm, if you can,
> poor in our openness.

That "openness" should be aligned with "poor" is an insight that calls to mind Emerson's severe and skeptical admonition in "Experience," that "We must hold hard to this poverty, however scandalous, and by more vigorous self-recoveries, after the sallies of action, possess our axis more firmly." Wallace-Crabbe, for all the toil and spin of his work, is like a gyroscope that never loses its balance.

Immersed in *Afternoon in the Central Nervous System*, you find yourself discovering another way of seeing and being that simply can't be replicated elsewhere. What makes this experience so pleasurable and also mystifying is that we have no easy frame of reference outside of it from which to judge or put it into perspective, no way to stabilize or render inert this flaring out of the mind so as to contemplate or even contradict it. As a result, Wallace-Crabbe demystifies the world for us, for as long as we are under his spell, and the intimation—or rather, the certainty—that we are in the presence of someone we cannot entirely comprehend or predict works to open us up to a freshness around us and to wonderment within:

> The dumb gene
> says nothing at all, but sits at home in my soul
> writing me still across its illiterate plan:
> a singular man chewing some general cabbage,
> looking out over the second millennium
> and feeling as fit as a trout.
> ["Afternoon in the Central Nervous System"]

His is constantly a poetry of surprise.

—Paul Kane

AFTERNOON IN THE
CENTRAL NERVOUS SYSTEM

We Being Ghosts Cannot
Catch Hold of Things

What a piteous quest we have
to brood upon down here

given that Meaning is a blind god
who limps through the actual world

seeking any attachment,
looking for good company.

Just on occasion one hears
the tap-tap-tap of his stick

or hers (it can hardly matter
thus far beyond all gender):

echoes that aim obliquely
at lovely natural things

which might, if wishes were horses,
be ever so gently handled and stroked

and Meaning at last
                    come home

in a susurrus of bay leaves.

Sunset Sky Near Coober Pedy

Streak, dash, fluff, apricot radiation,
the whorled blurring of a burned edge:
solid lavender continents and filiations,
islands in air, foolishly soft fleeces
dandled overhead, easterly pinks and peaches
nervously barred with mauve.
                              Dollop, smear,
streaking and massing, pos and neg,
versions of Crete, New Britain and the Coorong,
wool, flax, gelato, soapy froth
teasingly spread around like transient solids
over, behind, permeating or through.

They are done by drunken painters of genius
who, visited by vast hallucinations,
daubed them all over a monster's mural hall.
Some are like dried-out corpses glorified
or windblown spare parts of the heavenly host.
Their grammar escapes me.
                              The tune is hard to hear.
Powderblue, cream, blush, incandescent copper,
The meaning of what they are is merely IS.

Afternoon in the Central Nervous System

Eating raw cabbage at a paper-
littered table at autumn's end
I choose (or something chooses me) to read
an article about biology unclearly,
following in particular the Lamarckian
bit, the easy assault on Skinner
(everybody's enemy, I hope), the
anecdotes about Gregor Mendel's peas
and the delicate paths being traced
through the evergreen mind-body problem,
tracks over tricky terrain as dodgy
as those by which molecular adjustments
carry something from the senses cleanly back
to what I, of necessity, call Us.
We, whatever we are, keep wanting
to know how suppositious self in fact achieves
the confidence to keep slogging on
despite the madly random death of cells
and the rupture of connections.

Eating the noisy taste of cabbage while
a CD plays Debussy's *Iberia*
and ash leaves fall on the concrete slabs
of our backyard, I am bemused by how
the musing of the world thus chose me here
out of, say, Scottish tribes and the plaited rush
of history from Plato down to NATO.
Why omnivorous?
                    Why darkish-skinned?
And whence this quaint obsession with ball-games
as well as making verses? The dumb gene
says nothing at all, but sits at home in my soul

writing me still across its illiterate plan:
a singular man chewing some general cabbage,
looking out over the second millennium
and feeling as fit as a trout.

The Evolution Of Tears

I wonder whether grief was already invented
as far back as the Mindel and Wurm glaciations,
some rogue gene having tipped the scale.
                                        I wonder
whether the human creature was chosen by grief
as much as by stone tools or opposable thumb.
Did our hopeless remote forebear sit blubbing his eyes out
(her eyes?) by gunyah or cave? We just can't know.

Tears leave no grooves in archaeological sites,
a broken heart has never been troweled up;
the *lacrimae rerum* do not resemble objects
though misery be as hard as a stone in your hand.

A long way down the line were those other properties,
the lily of logic with a rose between her teeth,
privatization, debt, the barque of state
but grimmer human traits had crept in first
teaching the sad monosyllables, lost and gone.
One, more obscene, begins with a capital D.

Chemical? We comprehend grief, but not always:
a burial rips the guts out of everyone close.
We fail. We suffer. One slides into the ground
who had been a spirit, horsed round and laughed as we do
and now joins the majority . . .
                                        the tacit ones . . .
in a horizontal kingdom underfoot.
We do not understand.
                        Together we rise,
feather, turn and fly away.

Spranto Lost

Once on a time
Time was a language
Once on a time
Old everybody spoke
In god's Esperanto

Once in the language
They made a lot of bricks
A bric-a-brac of bricks
To stack and stick and stack
Way up to heaven

A tower in clouds
Aloud in the cloud
Stack rattle pop
And they all could speak
In god's Esperanto

Not happy, little men
Said the god like thunder
Booming broadly
Against that babble
Of people from Babel

So he broke their language
Like bits of firewood
And blew them all away
Across the desert
Of differing tongues

Off now they scattered
Camelback muleback
Misunderstanding
But yearning still for
The language umbrella

And The Cross

"Then their eyes were opened, and they recognized him;
and he vanished from their sight."

LUKE 24

Yes, it's a tale you've all heard bits of,
Whether in song or tranches of prose,
Clearly elsewhere in time and travel:
But what to make of it, God knows.

This is the family called Holy,
Not a typical Jewish name,
Who wrote their story sublimely through
Two millennia of fame.

She was with child by some Holy Spirit,
Not the easiest thing to say.
Joseph the carpenter recognized
That was where the future lay.

It was high time for the national census
Back in the town where he'd been born,
So off they went with hamper and donkey
Heading south, a little forlorn.

The electorate was Bethlehem;
Pubs and B & Bs were full.
They wanted somewhere better to stay
But didn't have the financial pull

So finished up in a straw-dry stable
With animals munching round about
But warm enough on a winter morning
As new-born Jesus now found out.

Three exotic astrologers
Had picked up good tidings, it appeared;
Out of the east they rode with their camels,
Each man sporting a different beard

And bringing presents for the baby,
Sweet-smelling frankincense and gold,
Also some other stuff called myrrh—
Whatever it is, you'll have to be told.

Shepherds guarding their flocks by night
Had seen a ruddy enormous star
And followed its path to the musty stable:
Sheep, donkey, shepherds, here they are.

It is all too easy for a mother
To think her baby the son of God
But Mary was gathered up in process,
Cornered by something extremely odd,

A junction in eastern history, say,
Or transcendental epiphany.
Also the time for visiting Egypt
(Without a side-trip to those fey

Pyramids or lion-women).
When things looked safer, home they came
Into father's traditional woodwork business:
Dailiness the name of the game.

Now the teenage years came rousing
The boy's vision; also his flair.
Gone missing, he was round at the temple
Kicking the shysters out of there.

Apart from tramping down to the river
And getting splashed by hairy John,
Nothing much happened until he was thirty:
A village carpenter's life went on

Toward that metaphor of the fisherman
Filling his little human creel
In definition contra the Romans,
Since all authority was unreal

Unless its meaning was that of spirit,
A medium we can't write down
Or freeze in marble. After thirty
He became the talk of the town,

In any gateway or market-square,
Rousing discomfort and interest.
(Remember that yarn of the good Samaritan
And hope it lingers in the West.)

Disturbances and transformations
Muscled the story toward its end
Which could be seen as a radiant beginning
By leper, prostitute or friend.

Read it as tragedy or his glory:
Nothing could be the same again.
Remember, he said to the Galilee fisherfolk,
I will make you fishers of men;

And then there had been such miracles,
Inaccessible to our age
But threads in the weave of a mental fabric—
Their Euro-Asian heritage.

His legacy? Make your own minds up.
Did Roman nails deserve his blood?
Even for someone who venerates money
Here is a story of absolute good.

Its Private Idiom

A room lies open
giving onto grasscolored silence,
the racket of our footsteps gone away

and the dust
which is friend to mankind
gathers over every thing inside

so that
when blue sky peeps in at breakfast-time
it sees the kindly coverlet of dust

like blessing
or a gray army blanket.

Sweet dust, bless us all in turn.
        Keep us warm, if you can,
poor in our openness.

The Shape-Changer

The first day he was traveling in Asia,
the next day he soared the flight of a wedge-tailed eagle,
the next day he was the gusting wind,
the next a bright campfire,
the next he thought of St. Kilda on those open, drifting, sleazy
    summer nights,
the next he was a seal, big-eyed and sleeky-brown,
next day the little cousin of Death
and the next a scaly writhing snake
or an ancient painted clock with two pewter soldiers to strike the
    hours,
the next day he stood with all the workers, shoulder to shoulder,
the next day he grew like a tree, covered with sunlight,
the next he was back swimming off Elwood under the stars, many
    years ago,
the next day he was a yellowish lion
and next the sandy, howling wind.

Being Proteus, he never dreamed at all.

Up At a Villa

So, it felt alright but now you rabbit on
expressing indisputable views on everything, in vivid
agreement with yourself, reinforcing the big Yes,
it having been determined that all popes and poets
can be no more than cocksuckers, arseholes, or merely both.
You smile with anger, red behind rimless glasses,
and right. Well, you could hardly be wrong, eh?
Even the pleasant CD cannot stem your fucking flow.
I wouldn't dare try, I tell you that.
Why is all this display of petty power so important
now to you: pretty well always has been. And why
does the furious cortex hunger after correctness,
in just about everything? Buggered if I know
but it must have been like this
ever since you swaggered out of your wicker cradle
and set about ruling the world; you had the measure
of left and right, art, money, sexual deviation
and all the main current of thought—
yes, I'll have another splash of red, why not.

Your garden flourishes outside in fruitful technicolor,
skillfully maintained, of course, by those expert hands
while you see through the cloudy glass of each political party
as well as the seamiest anti-Semites and mining thugs,
because you smell the due stink in everything,
the dirt that rots every pocket. Yes, you are bloody well like
those puritans you affect to hate so much, thin churchy rats.
Every phony, you force us to understand, has been fattened up
on taxpayers' money. No scholar is not a fake,
bar those few honest souls you happen to endorse
or at least agree with, today: those commonly known
as your disciples, docile ephebes and victims,
who wouldn't answer back in a month of Sundays.
We admire your dense green gardening, drink on,

nary a soul half-daring to answer back or argue—after all
who wants his or her noggin blasted off with a phrase
like fart-warmed thunder? Certainly not yours truly.
We'll go on laughing then into the deep lull of evening.
After all, tomorrow we're driving back to the city.

Erstwhile

Your girlfriend rang me up today,
your former girlfriend,
                    no, that isn't right,
the present friend of all that once was you,
your fetch or
what remains in the little photographs:
a boy in black-and-white
riding a horse into the scrub
or, freckled, reading out of doors,
both times T-shirted,
your hair a thick, dark bowl-cut
                    my erstwhile son.

Oh yes, she rang today,
had taken somebody out to see your grave
near the forked white trunk,
and we were sad together
on the phone, for a hard while
thinking of you, long gone now. Hence.

Where? Where are you?
In poor fact I can never come to grasp
the meaning of it all, supposing
that to be what religion's all about.
The loss remains behind
like never being well.

Father-In-Law

Alec, I said you'd be around
by stratagem or shift
looking for a lift
to the somewhere burial ground

where she and I had been
(who loved one another best)
laid to our earthbound rest
in that grassy, marbled scene.

Loving In Truth

Someone will push the house over one day,
Some spacedozer give it a shove,
But the cobbles we laid down here in the yard,
These are a labor of love.

All winter we set those cobbles in place,
Or was it the summer as well?
Sorting through lumpy bluestone pitchers
For ones that looked suitable.

The old house decayed—along with us—
Will a strange new resident
Admire the patio made in joy
Wondering what we meant?

Things fall apart, the poet wrote,
Certainties crumble or move
But the cobbles oddly plotted together,
Those are our labor of love.

An Die Musik

So repetition has its lovely place,
Being the engine-room of harmony
These ringing notes are all we know of grace.

Sound wings away and doesn't leave a trace,
The air vibrating with fragility,
But repetition has its lovely place.

Mere lives are dwindling at a carnal pace.
Given that gods are what we cannot see
These ringing notes are all we know of grace.

The planet slowly broils in pitchblack space;
You can't get back to the lawns of infancy
But repetition has its lovely place.

Time works at etching wrinkles on a face:
There's always pathos to our comedy.
These ringing notes are all we know of grace.

Listen: a texture delicate as lace
Repeats the long-gone master's melody.
These rising notes are all we'll know of grace
But repetition has its lovely place.

Introspection

Have you ever seen a mind
thinking?
It is like an old cow
trying to get through the pub door
carrying a guitar in its mouth;
old habits keep breaking in
on the job in hand;
it keeps wanting
to do something else:
like having a bit of a graze
for example,
or galumphing round the paddock
or being a café musician
with a beret and a moustache.
But if she just keeps trying
the old cow, avec guitar,
will be through that door
as easy as pie
but she won't know how it was done.
It's harder with a piano.

Have you ever heard the havoc
of remembering?
It is like asking
the local plumber
in to explore a disused well;
down he goes on a twisting rope
his cloddy boots
bumping against
that slimed brickwork

and when he arrives at bottom
in the smell of darkness,
with a splash of jetblack water
he grasps a huge fish,
slices it open
with his clasp knife
and finds a gold coin inside
which slips
out of his fingers
back into the unformed unseeing,
never to be found again.

Ode to Morpheus

It's a rum go, a pretty pickle, a rare kettle of fish
    that we spend so much of our time
(I will not say our days, those branchy olive intervals)
    rocking away in your arms: point-blank there.
Well, not as blank as that, but numbly a-wander
    along your tracks, your labyrinthine
halls through the great, ivied house that is
    always yourself in the long haul
studded with metamorphosis and yellow anticlimax—
    the wide, free mini-series of the night.

It seems pretty weird, oddball, queer as a coot
    that we switch off a third of our days
swaddled in linen, squeezed between counterpane
    and kapok; perhaps under doonas.
There was a bloke in the *Odd Spot* who somehow got by
    on 1.5 hours per night.
Was he smarter than us? We'll never suss it out
    but I resent like crazy all this
rehearsing for peace-without-end in our long last home.

It's a hard god, a crook umpy, a two of spades
    that figured our fortune out this way.
Instead of ranging the night, we snooze in your lap,
    the years ticking away like clockwork ducks
or hurdling the fence like sheep.
                    Fiddling the hints . . .
           sheedling the woolen flump . . .
                        Then, zzzz . . .

Last Page From an Explorer's Journal

Approaching from the south we lost Jacoby.
Alluvial soils gave out. The fevers went.
We climbed through furze toward the low bicuspids.
It was then, as I recall, that Dr. Spade
had trouble with the ponies and their harness.
Here and there anthracite came through the shale.
The whole thing is an ancient rift valley.
It was very dull.
     Tempers grew worse
until, that Wednesday, our track led round and up
to the east face, and we were in the Canines
which, with a sudden turnabout of weather,
gleamed high and jagged. Clouds brighter than snow
scarved them here. We ate small berries,
gathered campanula and woundwort. Murphy died of boils.

A Stone Age Decadent

Uh.

    Uh.

            These errant stripes of sun
That feather in play across my legs design
Transient ochres, ripples which the Sea
Has leant the air. I seem to like it here:
My tribal brothers work back up the stream
For tucker; one small knot of womenfolk
Go gathering shellfish where gold sand meets rock
There in the middle distance.

                    They compose quite well,
Sea-burnished nymphs and mothers with dry tongues.
Under these casuarinas on my slope
Of sandstone and soft needles I may hold
A laid-back peace, keeping my cavernous head
Well stocked with pictures.

                    Mm . . . hmmm. Let them retain
Their rules and moieties. I disturb no one,
Neither affront those boring Bluetongue rules
Nor trespass on Echidna's blunt decree

Here while a sea breeze lightly lifts my hair
Flavored with faint salt. Tribes are smart enough,
Let them think me no-hoper if they want to,
It troubles me no more than bushflies do
While thoughts waft up this hill: from here old Sea
Is crinkle-turquoise—rumpling, ruffled, white.
Gulls and swallows thread it.

           Uh.

              Sheer solitude
Watching these topmost branches bar sky's wink
With their shockhead tresses. This is my secret
Adaptation of totemic ground,

Sequestered high, brown half-shade where I lounge
Sending my spirit out to meet the Sea.
Fly, fine colorless bird, on thinky wings,
The words we use are only the words we're given;
They do not like to hear me saying that,
Preferring old songs, with their boom-bam-boom:

> *Here the big wave runs upon the shore.*
> *Here the spray blows up and up like smoke.*
> *Daily the shellfish, daily.*
> *Young girls gather foodstuffs by the white sands.*
> *At night the seagull has stopped crying.*
> *Daily the shellfish, daily.*

Totem and law, laws and unfair totems,
Banal, sublime, bestial, that's how
My fellow tribespeople make out the world.
Practical, sure enough—the food comes in—
But bone between the ears. At their sheer best
Witness down there, say, brownbeautiful but dumb.
Motes dance in light-slant just above my skin
And the glow-filled Sea shakes off her thousand colors
In tides of mystery.
                    Listen.
                          Gull and currawong
Sound their antiphon. How fast the shadows
Lengthen on sand, coarsen the hill-textures.
There is pleasure in it all if you sit still.

I do not think they like me very much,
Not even Moama with her small round breasts,
Scrub of light curls, pool eyes, fastmoving limbs
And buttocks I could cup in these two hands

And then . . . Oh-oh! It's much too pleasant,
That's to say painful, this line of thought.
Body responds. There! She stoops at the rocks.

I see only a single cloud today,
Thin, flattish, gray-white, drifting above the horizon.
All else says blue meets blue. And I relax
On springy casuarina needles here, my den
With a view. A spinebill's vivid uniform
Flushes to flowers a little down my slope.
I flex, reflect, withdraw.
                                        Ah me. We all
Must learn in a line of days to wither up
And die—or else die first. Just like the scallop,
Mussel, periwinkle, any living thing.

Ahi! Know something now. Am I a fly?

        Here the spray blows up and up like smoke.
        Daily the shellfish, daily.

Peer closely at these jointed leaves or branchlets,
Green fingers of skeletal hands
Knobbed with small tan knuckles. Just to stare
With care at this or that makes world seem good,
Be it spiky cones or multiply-scored bark.
I like it here. Those women on the sands
Make up a dance that fits a larger dance.
The bay, the hills contribute to my joy
As I do nothing. Ha. Yes. That's my game,
My hunt for needful store of images.
Lovely, yes, but what stuff underlies all?
What might all change mean? Are we like shellfish

To be shucked and eaten? Why does the great sun set?
I wonder how we tagged these words at all.
Life is more than animal grease and ochre.
I well might fall asleep . . .

Melbourne

Not on the ocean, on a muted bay
Where the broad rays drift slowly over mud
And flathead loll on sand, a city bloats
Between the plains of water and of loam.
If surf beats, it is faint and far away;
If slogans blow around, we stay at home.

And like the bay our blood flows easily,
Not warm, not cold (in all things moderate)
Following our familiar tides. Elsewhere
Victims are bleeding, sun is beating down
On patriot, guerrilla, refugee.
We see the newsreels when we dine in town.

Ideas are grown in other gardens while
This chocolate soil throws up its harvest of
Imported and deciduous platitudes,
None of them flowering boldly or for long;
And we, the gardeners, securely smile,
Humming a bar or two of rusty song.

Old tunes are good enough, if sing we must;
Old images, revamped *ad nauseam*,
Will sate the burgher's eye and keep him quiet
As the great wheels run on. And should he seek
Variety, there's wind, there's heat, there's frost
To feed his conversation all the week.

Highway by highway, the remorseless cars
Strangle the city, put it out of pain,
Its limbs now kicking feebly on the hills.
Nobody cares. The artists sail at dawn
For brisker ports, or rot in public bars.
Though much has died here, little has been born.

The Amorous Cannibal

Suppose I were to eat you
I should probably begin
with the fingers, the cheeks and the breasts
yet all of you would tempt me,
so powerfully spicy
as to discompose my choice.

While I gobbled you up
delicacy by tidbit
I'd lay the little bones
ever so gently round my plate
and caress the bigger bones
like ivory talismans.

When I had quite devoured the edible you
(your tongue informing my voice-box)
I would wake in the groin of night
to feel, ever so slowly,
your plangent, ravishing ghost
munching my fingers and toes.

Here,
       with an awkward, delicate gesture
someone slides out his heart
and offers it on a spoon,
garnished with adjectives.

The Bits and Pieces

"Swift's discovery, fundamental for art, is that there
are no uninteresting objects in the world so long as
there exists an artist to stare at everything with the
incomprehension of a nincompoop."
ANDREI SINYAVSKY

Artichoke
Children's drawings of trees
approximate you
with your striated trunk
and dense neat head
inflorescent
of purplish scales or flakes
for our buttery meals,
seeming a sort of edible pinecone,
a green knight's club
or else an absolute rose.

Banana
The lordly nutritious banana
is peeping over the crinkled rim
of some old pottery bowl or other
up on a sideboard,
                    at vantage:
look how his nose is black,
jetblack as lovebites that blotch
the yellow hide of his throat,
tropical patriarch
knowing perhaps
the new moon four days off.

Coffee
The waiter
unscrewed

his arm
at the elbow

and strong
black coffee
poured out
of his thumb.

Dodgems

Metallic beetles
hum round the polished rubber track
    in quest of fresh crashes.

Emus
It is
particularly
the particular way
they come
stepping
warily
down the path
in dark
wrinkled
stockings
and shabby
mini fur coats,
their weaving
Donald Duck
heads
ready
to dip
and snatch
your ice cream

that appeals;
this
and the way
they browse dumbly brown
in cattle-paddocks.

   Food
Back to the tangible, at least to food:
"Sake-marinated tempura prawns
on snowpea tendrils with wasabi
and ginger mayonnaise." Cripes!
And what would be for pudding, then,
sinker and cream, or apple compote?
I wonder how new cooks earn their stripes,
what they conceive as our ultimate good.

   Galvo
Those long gaunt shearing-sheds
on the long tilt of
               halfshaven hills
are built of it:
they are pastoral cathedrals
of dull rippled grey
or steely new ships of the soil
breasting against another winter gale
that fills the pines with whirling blackness.
The rustbrown battered stamping houses,
ovens of history
       in the bleached mountains
were made of it
when trolleys ran with quartz and gold.
Loosened sheets bang away
                     in yellow Januaries;
dark rotted pieces

                        lie in the creek's edge.
In the backyard
a creepergrown green dunny;
at the township's edge
threatening humpies of the defeated ones.
Galvanized iron
                        our modern thatch
for years you wore blue slogans
for Doctor Morse's Indian Root Pills
near this or that sequestered cowyard.

    Hair
Heaping, coruscating, a waterfall
light enough for the breeze to leaven,
this all too human foliage
to fill an amorous hand, a coffin
or the red eye of St. Paul.

    Ink
With scratches
splutterings
and with slow
predetermined blots
your thick fingers
learn to be learned
in it:
how to master
(Master Pupil)
the tyrannous
steel nib
into a painful
parade of copperplate
with no crossings-out
into a decent hand,

the linear
life of the mind.

    Jasmine
Honey sweetness of jasmine,
it bends up from the rickety paling fence
by untended beans and caulies.

Can such floods of scent
come from those frail starfish

bunched high on the tennis-court wire?
The gravel swoons,
the lobs drop back.

    Kelp
Slowly it blackens
on the yellow shore;
a hardness thickens
more and more

in leaf, bulb, flange
and rubbery stem
along the fringe
or scalloped hem
of surf-surge. Time
turns everything opaque,
including these

straps, grapes, trees,
fan, tress and rake.
Gone their soft prime.

Lavatory
Gets dubbed a toilet or
a washroom or
a bathroom or
just a dunny
recessively
unseen.

Matches
Pine soldiers in their horizontal
order of parade all day,
slender, boxed-in, regimental
each with his red beret.

Nectarines
From such rough barky trees
and crinkled crescent foliage they come
bearing the press of years
or boyhood's tang,
keen, heady, themselves,
not this nor that
keeping the seasons happily enough
and turning one crimson cheek
toward the embrace of sun.
Or sharp white teeth.

Opener
Is an astonishingly slim
metallic biped, that is if you call
Captain Ahab a biped;
knees together while
his two teeth bite down hard
if you twiddle his ears round and round
and he skates around the edge

of a silvery rink
on his head,
in his frustration
biting right through that tin crust.

    Passionfruit
Used to be plump and glossy
but his mackintosh has shrunk
as he sucks in his cheeks
while somewhere inside the room
he is giving you the pip
with a wonderfully sour sweetness
like last year caught in a daydream,
the tang of paradise.

    Quail
    Quail in a beer garden
brown behind netting
    shy as the long drinks pass.

    Roses
Theatrical trophies
bloodbright on their spiny butchered towers
this densely implicated origami
for whose soft host of kindred colors
language has no words
    (but surely there are phrases).

Curvaceous, heartfilled, polygonal cupcakes
when I bend to the table's vase
they slide away
into their rosy selves
    the one and the many.

Salt
We just can't do without it, watery friends,
acrid sodium chloride, the spice of our lives
adding that Certain Something as a poem does:
our mineral tang of wry intensification
used even by the scribeless tribes for money.
Lacking it, life would be insipid;
poetry zings on the lolling tongue
                    having crept up on you,
quiet as a glittering lizard
or the water swelling in at last
                    by parched banks.
Between these angular crystals and
their dark blue sea we live.

Telephone
Give me a presence, here to hand
that I might view and understand
but not encapsulated voice.

Bad magic this, a slice of noise
far from the circle of oneself.
(I wish it neither wit nor wealth . . .)
My truest image stands close round
breathing on Tom Tiddler's ground
and will not be distilled for sound.

Underwear
On the whole they have been much neglected,
especially by writers, these necessary smallclothes;
figuring as Linen in the eighteenth century
and vanished completely of course in the next,
in our own time they seldom score a mention
except as trashy erotic accoutrements

to be 'impatiently ripped away'
in the more boring kinds of fiction.

Give them their due: they do yeoman service
to our crotchly comfort, our body temperature,
cradling of boobs and ease of movement.
Whoever has fidgeted through a bad day
in awkward underpants knows the difference
they make to our psyche, and learns to praise
a technology which has learned to create them
light, resilient, airy and snug.

> *Volkswagen*
> It doesn't much matter to me
> that the motor has gone missing
> from your cutesy bug
> since you'll find a spare one
> tucked away in the boot.

> *Washing Machine*
> Behind a glass pane
> the wardrobe's wet personae
> play at vertigo.

> *X*
> You know that he is passing by
> just on the barely other side
> of marginal experience
> by heartstop, a breath on your neck,
> dim whiffs of garlic and old iron,
> the ceiling of your mouth gone dry,
> all fruits and leafage petrified.

Yams
It pleases me to think
of the humble yams
stacked in their market stall

ugly, knobbled clubs
of mediocre taste
lacking even

that noble mythology
which has grown around the spuds
of Sir Walter Raleigh

and a million bags of chips.
The yam has no glamour at all;
it merely lives in the world.

Zephyr
Yellowish, crumpled, frail,
the leafboats lie
on water black as pitch
under a marbling sky;
the secret wind moves through them
unseen but visible.

The Thing Itself

The important thing is to build new sentences,
to give them a smart shape,
get acquainted with grammar like a new friend.

One rubs down syntax
into a coarse familiarity,
such foreplay as closes down all thought.

Were it not
that the undertaking is too mannered
(as gnostic as a shower of rabbits)

I would go right back,
devising a sentence
unlike any such creature in creation;

like nothing on this planet:
a structure full of brackets and cornices,
twigs, pediments, dados and haloes and nimbs,

full of nuts, butter and flowers!
Sinewy, nerved,
capable of blotches or of waving hair.

That would be a sentence to really show the buggers,
like a cute
new thing

or like a tree
recently invented
by some utterly brilliant committee;

it would glitter, articulate,
strum and diversify.
It would be the thing itself.

Grasses

Sternly avoiding the asphalt, treading on grass
I pick my pernickety way across
this common urban transliteration of landscape,
the oddly broadcast parks and median strips,
saluting the god of grass with the rub of my feet:

feet which are held at bay by animal skins,
tanned, sewn, polished, and frequently scuffed.
Whitman wrote about your multiplicity
as leaves, and yet those thousands of blades are you,
billions, rather. Bland in your closepacked greenness,

your number exceeds those from whose fate you sprout.
Lushly after rain or wispily blond in summer,
bowing briefly you offer a carpet's welcome
still to the odd walker.
                    Lightly arriving
at a roundabout, I would choose the diagonal,

taking note of kikuyu, buffalo, bent and sedge,
feeling in touch, treading a kind of worship
or else, playing with language, my worship of kind.
Old Whitman thought you the hair of young dead men
but you whisper at my feet
                    that something will survive.

God

That is the world down there.
It appears that I made it,
but that was way back,
donkeys' years ago, children,
when I spoke like a solar lion
beguiling physics out of chaos.

I spun my brilliant ball in air.
Such thought was new to me
though I had not guessed at my lack
in the old indigo days,
children, before you fell—
to use a technical verb.

It is full of beautiful flair,
a jewel and a garden at once,
bluish-green with the track
of silver engraving its veins . . .
Shit, but it's lovely
and no end of trouble at all.

Children, it once was rough,
whatever the play of language,
with goats and bladderwrack,
with banksia trees and wrens.
I endeavored to bring it up rich.
I reckon it's my museum.

I gave a big party
and the name of the party
kept slipping clean away

from my wooden tongue
but I reckon it was
called history.

Some honored guests
took off their names
or left them impaled like scarecrow rags
on my stagy front hedge.
I thought of it as being
a party for my son.

A Barbarian Catechism

No, dear friend,
I don't have a full heart
for all the Christian stock and barrel, but
with half a mind still need
much of it some of the time, at least until
something more serious
comes along, which hasn't happened yet.
Epiphanies are for real, given
that "man isn't equally moral all the time"
according to clever, dangerous
Nietzsche, who liked to say he was really Polish,
not a goofy German,
and declared that Christianity came along
in order to lighten the heart.

So Christmas is hard to get away from still,
despite the cards and toys,
those haunting carols again and again calling back
our own childhood as well
as His, an absolutely important
child in a wintry manger,
prickly with straw, whether he was
the child of God, like us
or seriously different. Yes, he died in the spring,
which was autumn down here in Australia,
but his sacrifice has got muddled with rabbits and eggs.
Again, I am pretty dodgy
about angels and saints, while the life everlasting
is an awesome whatnot which
just keeps on changing utterly all the time.
Grace I can understand;
it would make sense to a perfectly heathen soul

and so might Blessing.
      Indeed, lacking grace, how could we endure
the painfulness of days.

For these, for all the incomparable stories,
      tall articulate churches
and Piero della Francesca's "Baptism of Christ,"
      I give wholehearted thanks
and bless a tradition that sheds a various light
      like stained-glass windows.

Puck Disembarks

That sun is glazing and glaring in the wrong direction.
In his government regulation gear
And cultural arsy-turvitude
Puck steps ashore in a grammar of ti-tree.
    He rocks the pinnace.
    The foliage looks pretty crook.

Even a spirit can fail to be gruntled
Standing on his northern hemisphere head
In a wilderness without fairies or dairies,
Whose Dreaming he cannot read.
    He tweaks a tar's pigtail.
    This land is all wombat-shit.

The mosquitoes lead him to think of swallows,
The dipping swallows of Devon
And these alien magpies can sing like Titania
In love with a kangaroo.
    Puck waters the rum,
    Peddling the balance to snubnosed natives.

The glittering wavelets throw on yellow sand
Big shells like Wedgwood ware
As the imp rises inside him, getting ready
To rewrite Empire as larrikin culture.
    He daubs a first graffito on
    The commissary tent, GEORGE THE TURD.

Against the pale enamel sky
Rebel cockatoos are screaming
New versions of pleasure:
This is the paradise of Schadenfreude.
    He begins to adore
    The willy wagtail's flirting pirouettes.

Mozart on the Road

"The sensibility of his organs appears
to have been excessive."

THE BOOK OF DAYS

Too much of his childhood
would have been bumped and sloshed away
in a post-chaise or damp coach
between indescribable towns
or jammed into yet another
unsewered inn. Not good

for a bright boy growing up.
What could he have been doing
on the slow road between, say,
Schitzberg and sodden Krappfeld?
Would he and Nannerl have found
word games to make up?

It must all have played
merry hell with his constitution,
yet his mind worked away
like a Stakhanovite
through many a traffic jam
or when some new board displayed

notice that the bridge
not far ahead was down.
And what did he take for his colds?
Did Leopold bring a flask
of eau-de-vie? All such travel
was far from a privilege.

Travel narrows the mind,
one is often tempted to say,
but he was quick as a flash,
impressions through muddy windows
metamorphosing into
harmonies unconfined

by the curiosity
of rude, stinking, scruffy postilions.
All this flowed into a thought-voice
which evoked such terrible yearning
that nothing but itself
could ever satisfy.

Robert Browning at Bundanon

There's a kookaburra chortling, so I think it's time for tea.
That's a cup in bed for you, then, and another one for me.
We'll have a day devoted to creative enterprise,
you exploring with a paintbrush and, after several tries
I could come up with something: not quite burned out, after all;
might hatch a crafty lyric handling chaos and Man's fall,
but locating this among the valley's kangaroos and cows
with a special spot for wombats.
                Around the lower boughs
fantails are finding insects, swallows fossick for their food.
Business bastards keep insisting profit is the only good;
old Galluppi's out of fashion; Philip Glass is all the go,
but any income from our art seems incrementally slow,
poet or painter.
          How the Brangus bellow there,
wanting hay forked out for breakfast in the dewy atmosphere.

Who was it, I wonder, first contrived the electric fence
those cattle keep away from? They are not entirely dense.
Nor am I, one keeps on hoping, though absurdly out of date
with a weather-eye for verse forms, fanciful and intricate.
What'll we do with the mystical, a question for us all
in an age way past King Arthur, Joan of Arc and bold Ben Hall,
when the shadows of religion are like birdcalls in the bush
and mammon jingles loudest.
              There's a wattlebird now—whoosh!

The Speech of Birds

That there should now
be red berries down there
to the left of third-big-tree
will concern me later

for now I know
plentiful grass seeds are eating-ready
near fence and far enough
from cat

and even before that
I'll pick up
those excellent lengths of straw
just the shot

for home repairs
a bit closer though
to big cat prowling ground

Four legs more dangerous
two more or less benign
but upstairs in our tree

those bloody wattlebirds
and squealing gangs of lorikeets
could drive one crazy

Some days I can't even hear
a melodious lovesong
from down the way

nor the clamant warning
that sparrowhawk is hovering now
somewhere above leafless

riding the breath of death

From the Island, Bundanon

Eight stones lie on my trestle desk,
three cream-striped with injected quartzite,
one a very plain gray segment
for the moon goddess, three pebblesized
white, ginger and lustrous black; the last
a pocked palmful of sandstone.
River-rubbed, they fall into design.

Muscular underachievers with big brainpans,
Neanderthals dawdled on in the west of Europe
until that corner caught up with the rest of us
then nicked on smartly, ahead for centuries
or more, playing tricks with bright metal and glass.
Where are the old values?
What became of those big blokes and their women?

Unknowable, they fall into design,
stars that all peoples have known
by cluster-name, and flowing down the sky
a Milky Way: the whole beyond belief,
altogether impossible,
                              yet across them drags
the flickering of two planes bound for Melbourne.

Why is mistletoe so droopingly widespread
in this country, so distant indeed
from Sir J. G. Frazer's multinational magic?
Is it a marsupial kissing-bough
trailing its tressage of scimitars and bullets
in parody on a parent eucalypt?
The bush is hospitable to such festoons.

The brown rocksolid wombat
that has a dithering habit
neither thunders away
nor gets around to diving
into his well-dug bolthole
but pauses in dusty fur
to consider all the options.

Urban *they* remain quite as desiccating
as the dear little sachet of calcium chloride
you find in a chemist's bottle. They
have no response to the way the lower
squadron of windblown cloud
rushes past us, dynamically indifferent
to the marbled welkin above.

Innocent cylinder with a wound,
you have kept the grape's rich blood
from the disillusioning breath of day
at your own cost. Freckled and branded
you lie here on the table,
one end pale magenta. Far from your tree
you became pleasure's sacrifice.

Scar tissue earned from shorts and dead lantana
mapping that stony island
has left a cartography of signs
all over both shins, generously so.
Like stars or complicated cells
they look to spell a meaning I can't read,
inescapably riverine.
                    And rough.

To make, said Hardy, the clock of years
turn backward, I might enter then
a decade when there was my father
and I could know my eldest son
in his plight, but these are dream
as I shuffle the stones on my writing desk
and the stars whirl in endless night.

Timber

When the pearly rain
            comes pelting in at this angle
and the dark stringybark branches
            look brittle and dangerous
you roundly un-Heathcliff yourself
            so as to head
                        for creature comforts.

            And then the question rises:
could there be
            a book that really would
set everything at ease?
            Even the Holy Bible
hasn't managed it yet
            not even on its better days.

What is it
            that other people do?
Could they describe
            the taste of spring water
evocatively?
            And we do have to wonder
In whose fluent mind
                        history gets made
embryonically.

Like most of you
I'm obliged to say
            that it wasn't me,
not for worlds.

II

Against the blue, against the whatsoever,
a tower of poplar has been lashing away
like damaged birds.

Some blown demon has to invade my life
shorting all the circadian rhythms and buffeting me aside.
Body inhabits a throbbing
or some vice-versa, crudely at odds with time.
Is a brainstorm plus or minus?

The westward sky behind that heaving tree
Is dirty pearls.
                        Nothing short
of a cold whalebreath of wind
skims in from chaos,
turning personality outside in.

Nowhere is everywhere by now.

III

The tousled children
have their own way
                        with trees,
                        their own classification:

How is this one to climb?
Are the branches handy enough?
What about splinters and thorns?

Their aim
a perfect lookout
                    or lofted cubby house
in dense leafage,
close to the old gods.

IV

In boyhood there was fascination with mallee roots,
no objects on our planet
seemed less geometrical. They were
the purely organic, naturally baroque.

Yet in a neighboring woodyard they were stacked
in an enormous cube,
a solid brown rick
of culture working on still life.

We bought them. Just a few.
        And they burned for us.

V

A dark season lurked
        in the middle of that summer;
I labored with pen
        and pencil, axe and hammer.

While chopping on the slope
        I cracked a short log open
And saw a glossy cricket
        squat on the wood, unshaken;

at first he would not budge:
    when I came back he had gone,
had crawled off into dry grass
    and summer's heat came on.

VI

Lingered smell of Scotch pine,
aromatic as a bunch of lavender,
stars bursting through jagged branches
and little tags of resin
    sticky on both my hands.

VII

The shouldering ash-tree,
close, greenfeathery, witch-encumbered,
was felled at eleven today.

A tree-man shinned slowly up
the living trunk
riding on spiked boots

or futuristic gaiters.
Big branches came stripping away,
Each with a soft crash.

A white snow of nuptial sawdust
lies across the backyard.

The sky can get at us now,
more and more stars in my hair.

VIII

Alone, in coffeecolored twilight
you gravely turn back
to unresponsive others:
granite, water and wood.

Wood is the hand's old friend
as club, or careworn grip
into a rocking green treetop,
grainy for tool or sport.

Split redgum can cry
splinteringly to the heart
or a whippy branch whistle through air,
the life still in it.

When I smell timber
it flows inside me;
touching an edge, I feel
the coarse flesh of all being;

but in a stand or copse
of windlashed alterity
I might now also hear
the first gods murmuring.

IX

Ebony, balsa, oak, mahogany,
    bo-tree, ti-tree, pepperina,
        red cedar, blackwood, Glastonbury thorn,
    hemlock, mulga, sandalwood, yew . . .

Rondo

Over the steady, littoral ground bass one sees that
our ocean has four natty trims of lace.
Container ships go by like rectangles.
Motor cars down there are barely awake.

        . . . be still now

Wren and honeyeater pay visits occasionally to
the outrageously national agapanthus,
surely a weed, though, in its near-violet profusion.
Sun butters at least selective bluegum trunks while
birds around are speaking myriad languages,
most of them urgently:
one sounds a keen mechanical bell, to what end?

        . . . try to stay calm

Holiday houses still have chains across the drive.

Acoustically, cockies tear their sheets of steel
when they're not competing for bird-table preference.
But look down the bosky slope, now:
a few more sedans trace the S-bend and small bridge
on their way to some other bay
where the foreshore has also been colonized
by a million toothy dandelions;
big cats live somewhere else again.

        . . . be still, my heart.

Remorseless bass of big surf carries on.

Fire Doom

The bushfires rant around our draggled town
Disintegrating some bloke in his house
And broiling others, where sedans broke down
Blindly. All blackened, from wombat to mouse.

That moment screamed in, rumored to be like
Four Lockheeds or Rolls Royces in your head.
If you still have a head, now. The melted bike
Squats on the ash: one charger for the dead?

Nature must lack the chivalry we'd sniff
As brotherly tribute: something has turned out worse
With Plato's cave become a blazing cliff.

Pain is the knot-hole in our universe
And yet the black calligraphy of trees
Can make this long view elegantly Chinese.

Rendition

Not, please, this creeping elaborate pain
and not slow parody of how lives end,
not policemen in mufti playing a dirty god,
not the stinking underside of Elsewhere,
regime of colonels or generals or psychopaths,
not fascination with just how far a body can be made to go
nor the treatment of survival as precisely equal to dying.

Please, not a hammering on the door at three in the morning;
not, I'm afraid, you're going to have to come with me.
Not the large plain dull old car
waiting outside your front door with motor grumbling
for the quick take-off,
nor the bareness of a shabby room with overbright lighting.
Not Them, moving in.

Certainly not having to take off your clothes;
water, the truncheon, the cold, the blaring, the slaps
and long standing still in one damned place,
not the prodded humiliation of your nudity,
clothed ones treating you as a slab of meat,
not the drawn-out thickness of questioning
and not the detumescence of hope.

Not the naked genitals like frightened mice,
not something hard inserted in the vagina,
not pints of liquid trickled down your throat,
not a bully's foul breath up against your face
as concentration goes,
not the pummeled phonebook against your guts
leaving no distinct bruises.

Not the electrodes.

Fuck, no, not the electrodes
and not your buttocks beaten, then beaten again,
not something pushed right up under your fingernails
nor a bloody gobbet hacked off your left ear—
which you are then going to be forced to eat.
Not weeks without food.

Bodies have been designed frail, by and large, by and small
ready to be tormented and taken apart.
The shit may run down your cold legs.
You may die.
You will suffer and die.
You will survive, language holding some trace of you for years,
and the mourners, too.

The Stone's in the Midst of All

Little by little
things have been passing over me,
liquid, furry, ephemeral
slowcoach aeons and banks of cloud.
There have been good and bad millennia
                 according to some principle or other.

Sometimes I shift a bit
but mostly just lie around
while happening happens to others
who then go away.
                 Soon enough:
it's hard to know what they were there for.

So here I am
                 and abide
taking things pretty much as they come,
different from the fickle weather,
set in my ways but
gaining a certain polish.

And our speculative humans, lairy
with all their bundles of hubbub,
                 their brief diversity,
drift clean away.

        Remember those worthy Neanderthals?
Gone with the long wind.

In the Scent of Eucalyptus

Full midnight shows her out there after all,
a gardener at midnight, unencumbered
by all the miscellaneous junk of day,
secateurs, fork and sensible straw hat
                              against freckling,
big moon scudding now through argosies
and then coming clear,
        absolutely marvelous the way
it does the whole mise-en-scène silver and depthless dark
so you can't even tell
                    tristanias from gums, or apple trees,
all dipped in some Indian ink,
nor can you make out the color of her jumper
where she walks on the toes of dramatic shadow,
drawing it across lit turf, by gardenbeds
                            and a snaky hose
all done in the Great Printmaker's black-and-white,
seemingly frozen silent,
only the eye of Mars a little red.

Flowing

That small rock sketches herringbone
                forms on the stream
and his poems were so full of joy
        you hardly would dream
that the steady encroachment of death
        was his usual theme.

ACKNOWLEDGMENTS

Most of the works here were previously collected in my *New and Selected Poems*, published by Carcanet Oxford Poets in 2013. My grateful response is thereby made to my patient, kindly editors at Carcanet, in Manchester. "Up at a Villa" has recently appeared in *The Best Australian Poems 2013*, edited by Lisa Gorton (Black Inc); "And the Cross" in *PN Review*; "Rondo" and "And the Cross" have been published in *My Feet Are Hungry* (Pitt Street Poets, Sydney, 2014); while "Rendition" was a *Guardian* Poem of the Week last year. Several of these poems have also been published in *The turnrow Anthology of Contemporary Australian Poetry* (ULM, Monroe, Louisiana), edited by John Kinsella. I would like to express my especial gratitude to Paul Kane for seeing this book into being and through the press.

Chris Wallace-Crabbe is the renowned author of more than twenty collections of poems. His most recent books of verse include *Telling a Hawk from a Handsaw* (Carcanet Oxford Poets), *New and Selected Poems* (Carcanet Oxford Poets) and *My Feet are Hungry* (Pitt Street Poets). The founding chair of Australian Poetry Limited, he is Professor Emeritus at the University of Melbourne. Wallace-Crabbe has spent time in India and has taught at Harvard University and the University of Venice, Ca' Foscari. His awards include the Dublin Prize for Arts and Sciences, the Christopher Brennan Award for Literature, the Philip Hodgins Memorial Medal, and the Order of Australia. A public speaker and commentator on the visual arts, he specializes in artists' books.